This book is due for return on or before the last date shown below.

1 5 OCT 2009

1 7 MAR 2011   - 4 JUL 2017

2 6 SEP 2011

1 0 OCT 2011

2 7 FEB 2012

- 1 MAR 2012

2 3 APR 2012

- 8 M OCT 2012
1 5 APR 2013

1 0 JUN 2016

LIVES IN CRISIS

The Civil Rights Movement

NIGEL RITCHIE

HODDER
Wayland

an imprint of Hodder Children's Books

Published in Great Britain in 2002 by
Hodder Wayland, an imprint of Hodder Children's Books.

This book was prepared for Hodder Wayland by Ruth Nason.

Series concept: Alex Woolf
Series design: Carole Binding

British Library Cataloguing in Publication Data
Ritchie, Nigel
   The civil rights movement. - (Lives in crisis)
   1.Civil rights movements - United States - History
   I.Title
   323'.04'0973

ISBN 0 7502 3639 6

Printed in Hong Kong by Wing King Tong

Hodder Children's Books
A division of Hodder Headline Limited
338 Euston Road, London NW1 3BH

Cover (left) and page 1:
Martin Luther King at the final rally of the 'March against Fear', at the Mississippi State Capitol, June 1966.

Acknowledgements

The Author and Publishers thank the following for their permission to reproduce photographs: Corbis/Bettmann: pages 6, 7, 16b, 18, 21, 22b, 24, 25, 27t, 27b, 33, 34, 36, 38, 45, 47, 48, 56, 57; Corbis/Morton Beebe S. F.: page 51; Corbis/ReutersNewmedia Inc.: pages 5, 59; Corbis/Flip Schulke: cover/page 1, page 42; Corbis/Joseph Sohm; ChromoSohm Inc.: page 52; Corbis/Ted Streshinsky: page 44t; Corbis/Peter Turnley: page 54; Peter Newark's American Pictures: cover (right)/page 3 and pages 9, 11t, 11b, 12, 13, 14t, 15t, 15b, 16t, 22t, 37, 44b; Popperfoto: pages 4, 14b, 19, 20, 23, 28, 29, 30, 31t, 35, 39, 41, 43, 46, 50, 53t, 53b, 58.

CONTENTS

Black parents and children demonstrate
against school segregation in Saint
Louis, early 1960s.

THE LITTLE ROCK CRISIS

For a Southern town, Little Rock, Arkansas, was considered progressive. Many public facilities were desegregated, including the libraries and parks. Following a 1954 Supreme Court ruling, which declared separate schools for blacks and whites to be unconstitutional, the local school board had adopted a gradual desegregation plan. When term started on 4 September 1957, nine black students were to become the first in the state to attend a white high school.

National Guards turn away Elizabeth Eckford as she approaches Little Rock Central High School, September 1957.

However, as in most Southern states, there was little local support for the Supreme Court's judgement. Sensing the popular mood and citing the need to prevent disorder, the Arkansas state governor, Orval Faubus, sent in the National Guard to surround the school on 3 September. He warned, 'Blood will run in the streets if Negro pupils should attempt to enter Central High School.'

That night, Daisy Bates, president of the local branch of the National Association for the Advancement of Coloured People (NAACP), was busy arranging for all nine students to travel to school together. She called eight of them, but forgot to send a message to Elizabeth Eckford, whose home had no telephone. In the morning, the eight students were driven to the school under police escort. They were denied entry and went away.

Meanwhile, Elizabeth got off the bus a block away from the school and felt reassured when she saw the National Guard outside. A crowd of people followed her towards the school entrance, taunting and jeering, but she walked up to a guard who she had just seen letting in some white students. He blocked her way, raising his bayonet. When she tried to squeeze past, other guards joined him. The crowd continued to threaten her as she made her way back to the bus stop.

Faces in the crowd

Elizabeth Eckford described what happened when she approached the guards outside the school:

'They glared at me with a mean look and I was very frightened and didn't know what to do. I turned around and the crowd came toward me … somebody started yelling, "Lynch her! Lynch her!" I tried to see a friendly face somewhere in the mob … I looked into the face of an old woman and it seemed a kind face, but when I looked at her again, she spat on me. They came closer, shouting, "No nigger bitch is going to get into our school. Get out of here!"

… then I looked down the block and saw a bench at the bus stop … When I finally got there … I sat down and the mob began shouting all over again ... Just then a white man sat down beside me, put his arm around me and patted my shoulder. He raised my chin and said, "Don't let them see you cry". Then, a white lady … put me on the bus and sat next to me. She asked my name and tried to talk to me, but I don't think I answered. I can't remember much about the bus ride …'
(Quoted in Carson, *The Eyes on the Prize: A Civil Rights Reader*)

1999: along with the other eight former students, Elizabeth Eckford receives a Congressional Gold Medal from US President Bill Clinton, in recognition of their heroism and the pain they suffered in the cause of civil rights.

Two weeks later, after a private meeting with US President Eisenhower, Faubus withdrew the National Guard. An unruly mob took their place. So on 23 September, the nine black students, who had still not taken their classroom places, were smuggled into the school by city police. When word got out that they were in the school, a riot broke out and the police had to smuggle them out again before they were lynched.

Newspaper and TV reports of these events made Little Rock the focus of national attention. The situation was presented as a test of power between the federal (US) and state (Arkansas) governments. Southern Congressmen had already publicly attacked the Supreme Court ruling as an attack on states' rights. The question now was whether the federal government would intervene to uphold that ruling.

At a press conference, after US paratroopers were sent in to Little Rock, Governor Faubus accuses President Eisenhower of 'police state tactics'.

Escape

Melba Pattillo Beals recalled what happened after the students had been smuggled into the school on 23 September:

'What I felt inside was terrible, wrenching, awful fear ... I'd only been in the school a couple of hours and by that time it was apparent that the mob was just overrunning the school ... We were trapped ... Even the adults ... were panicked ... someone made a suggestion that if they allowed the mob to hang one kid, they could then get the rest out. A gentleman, who I believed to be the police chief, said, "Unh-uh, how are you going to choose? You're going to let them draw straws? ... I'll get them out."

... And we were put in two cars ... This guy revved up his engine and he came up out of the bowels of this building, and as he came up ... I could hear the yelling, I could see guns, and he was told not to stop.'
(Quoted in Hampton and Fayer, *Voices of Freedom*)

Eisenhower addresses the nation

On 24 September, President Eisenhower went on nationwide television to explain why he was using federal troops:

'Our personal opinions about the decision have no bearing ... Mob rule cannot be allowed to override the decisions of our courts ... the foundation of the American way of life is our national respect for law.'
(Quoted in Vexler, *Dwight Eisenhower: Presidential Documents*)

Faced with the most serious challenge to federal authority since the Civil War, President Eisenhower reluctantly intervened, placing the state National Guard under his direct command and sending in 1,000 paratroopers to escort the black students into school. A week later, after the troops were withdrawn, the children's troubles really began. Now they had to endure the daily torments of a hostile school.

The nine students make their way to the army station wagon which took them to and from school, October 1957.

The daily struggle

For the Little Rock Nine, the real battle was fought out of range of news cameras and reporters, during the school year. Ernest Green and Melba Pattillo Beals recalled those days:

'They'd taunt you in the corridors, try to trip you, throw ink at you ... You'd get phone calls at night, saying they'd have acid in the water guns and squirt it in our faces. You'd be crazy not to be scared.'

'... you start to understand your own ability to cope no matter what. That is the greatest lesson I learned.'
(Quoted in Hampton and Fayer, *Voices of Freedom*)

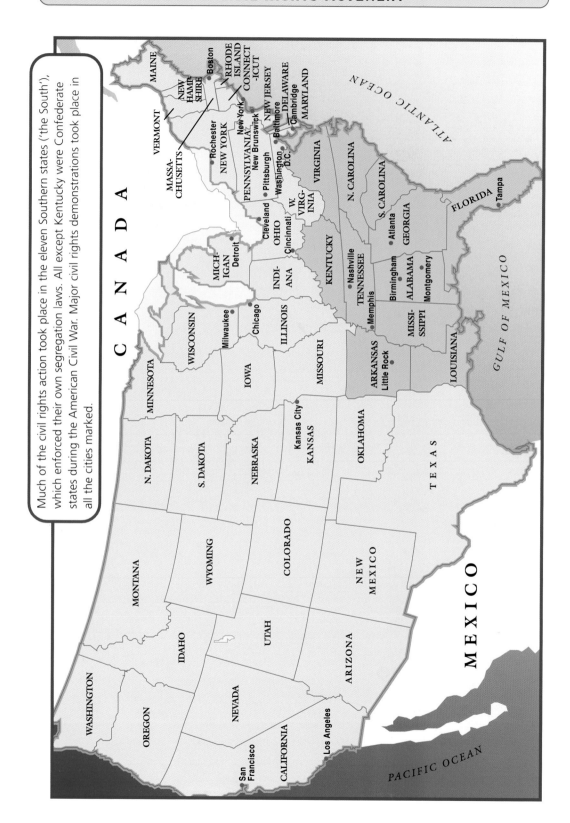

Much of the civil rights action took place in the eleven Southern states ('the South'), which enforced their own segregation laws. All except Kentucky were Confederate states during the American Civil War. Major civil rights demonstrations took place in all the cities marked.

SLAVERY, SEGREGATION AND CIVIL RIGHTS 1619–1954

Until the 1960s, segregation and discrimination were facts of life for most blacks living in the Southern states of the USA. However, in the mid-1950s, a civil rights movement appeared that challenged this inequality, using boycotts, marches and other forms of non-violent resistance to persuade the government to change the laws. Although politicians and judges helped speed the process, it was the courage and support of thousands of ordinary people that produced the biggest transformation in post-war American society. They forced the government to recognize (in law at least) equality (including fair trial, protection from discrimination, and the vote) for all citizens, regardless of their skin colour.

Slavery

Most black Americans are descended from African slaves, who were transported to the American colonies from the

A slave auction in Richmond, Virginia, 1856.

seventeenth century onwards to work on plantations run by white settlers. Slaves were treated as private property, being bought and sold like animals. White people justified slavery by claiming racial superiority and arguing that blacks were unfit for 'civilized society'.

In 1776, representatives of the American colonies drew up an ambitious Declaration of Independence (from Britain), which included the words, 'We hold these truths to be self-evident, that all men are created equal, that God has given them rights which cannot be taken away. Among these are life, liberty and the pursuit of happiness.' After the War of Independence had been won, slavery continued in the South, where plantation owners depended on slave labour for the profitable cultivation of cotton. So the new American constitution wrote slavery into the law, declaring that for purposes of taxation and representation, each slave would count as three-fifths of a person. However, many people in the North disapproved of

A war of words

Two extracts from the 1830s set out the positions of the pro- and anti-slavery camps. From a speech given by the governor of South Carolina:

'We need answer only to God for slavery. And slavery clearly has his blessing. The African Negro is destined by Providence for slavery. It is marked on his skin and by his lack of intelligence and ability to care for himself. They are in all respects inferior to us. They are not able to cope with freedom ...'

From a book by Theodore Dwight, a preacher:

'Slaves are treated like animals. They are overworked, underfed, badly clothed and housed ... They are forced to wear chains, iron collars with prongs ... they have their teeth torn out, they are flogged and have salt rubbed in their cuts. If they run away they are hunted down like dogs, whipped, branded, maimed, mutilated and more.'
(Quoted in Kelly, *Black Peoples of the Americas*)

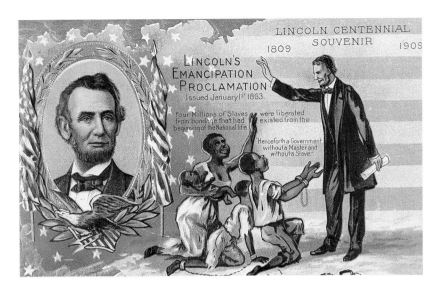

A postcard commemorating the 100th anniversary of the birth of Abraham Lincoln.

slavery and, in 1831, white liberals founded the Abolitionist movement to campaign for its end. The Abolitionist debate went on for 30 years in pamphlets, meetings and newspapers, reflecting the growing differences between 'slave' and 'free' states.

A black Union army soldier with his wife, c. 1865.

The Civil War, Reconstruction and segregation

In February 1861, ten Southern states, fearing the growing anti-slavery movement in the North, left the Union to set up their own Confederate States of America. The Republican president, Abraham Lincoln, refused to let the Union be broken up in this way, and war was declared. When Lincoln issued the Emancipation Proclamation in 1863, freeing slaves in the 'rebel' states to fight for the Union cause, it was more a question of military convenience than a commitment to equal rights. But soon after the North's victory in April 1865, slavery was formally abolished throughout the USA with the passing of the 13th amendment (to the Constitution).

The price of freedom

After gaining their freedom, many slaves found themselves working in the same conditions as before for the same masters. Patsy Mitchner recalled:

'Slaves prayed for freedom, got it and didn't know what to do with it. Slavery was a bad thing. But the freedom they got, with nothing to live on. That was bad, too ... Lots of masters took them back ... I bin working for white folks, washing and cooking, ever since freedom came.' (Quoted in Kelly, *Black Peoples of the Americas*)

Freedom was not the same as equality, however, and blacks required two further amendments (the 14th and 15th in 1866 and 1870) before they could enjoy full citizenship and voting rights. During the Reconstruction years after the Civil War, many blacks were elected to state and national offices.

A cartoon published in 1874 comments on the plight of blacks in the South after the Civil War.

However, little was done to help the slaves 'reconstruct' their daily lives. A Freedman's Bureau provided schools and work, but hardly any practical assistance, such as land or tools. Share-cropping now replaced slavery, as former slaves 'rented' small patches of land in return for a share of their crop, and many 'freedmen' soon found themselves indebted to their former masters.

By 1877 Reconstruction had collapsed, after Southern resistance persuaded the North to withdraw its troops and Southerners regained control of their state governments. New state laws ignored the amendments, removing all the newly gained black rights. Much of the resistance stemmed from the activities of the Klu Klux Klan (KKK), a secret society founded in 1865 and devoted to white supremacy. For four years its members rode around in their 'uniform' of white robes and pointed hoods, whipping, burning and murdering thousands of blacks. Those who had managed to buy their own land were soon forced off it.

After the KKK was disbanded in 1869 (for being too violent!), the violence continued, with over 3,000 lynchings between 1880 and 1918. Fear of physical intimidation kept many Southern blacks 'in their place' and whites committed murder, knowing that they would not be punished.

In 1896, the highest court in the land confirmed the legality of segregation. When Homer Plessy (seven-eighths white) was arrested for riding in the 'whites only' section of a Louisiana train, he sued the railway company for violating his right to equal citizenship under the 14th amendment. The Supreme Court disagreed, stating that segregation was legal if separate facilities were 'substantially equal' – and this 'separate but equal' doctrine lasted for almost 60 years. In practice, black facilities were grossly inferior. Following this decision, 'Jim Crow' laws (named after a black minstrel in a popular song) extended segregation in the South across a wide range of public services, including parks, libraries and even blood banks.

Members of the Klu Klux Klan, 1868.

'Our Constitution is color-blind'

On 6 May 1896, eight out of nine members of the Supreme Court supported the Plessy v. Ferguson ruling. The lone dissenter, Justice John Harlan, condemned the decision's consequences:

'Our Constitution is color-blind ... The destinies of the two races, in this country, are indissolubly linked together, and the interests of both require that the common government of all shall not permit the seeds of race hate to be planted under the sanction of law.'
(Quoted in Wexler, *The Civil Rights Movement: An Eyewitness History*)

No progress without struggle

From the 1840s, Frederick Douglass toured the country speaking out against slavery and oppression. In a speech in New York in 1857, he said:

'If there is no struggle there is no progress. Those who profess to favour freedom and yet depreciate agitation, are men who want crops without ploughing up the ground... This struggle ... may be both moral and physical; but it must be a struggle. Power concedes nothing without a demand.' (Quoted in Wexler, *The Civil Rights Movement: An Eyewitness History*)

The first black leaders

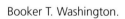

Booker T. Washington.

Meanwhile, blacks were finding their own voice to campaign against these injustices. The first great black leader was Frederick Douglass (1817-95), an escaped slave. Teaching himself to read and write, he became a leading anti-slavery and civil rights campaigner from the 1840s, promoting the cause through public meetings and a weekly paper, *The Northern Star*. Douglass also championed women's and workers' rights and held several government posts after the Civil War.

The leadership vacuum created by Douglass's death was filled by Booker T. Washington (1856-1915), another ex-slave, who became unofficial adviser to two presidents. White supremacy in the South was so established by 1900 that Washington urged blacks to accept the status quo and work from within. He argued that there was no point in demanding political progress until they had made economic progress.

As head of a black educational institute in Alabama, Washington vigorously promoted his policy of economic self-help through vocational training (such as carpentry, farming and domestic service). Hard work (rather than voting or better education) was the key to getting black people accepted as equals. Immensely popular in the South, he was a controversial figure to many Northern blacks, who criticized his programme for reinforcing white notions of superiority.

1910: an algebra class at the Tuskegee Industrial Institute, founded by Booker T. Washington.

In the North, the 14th and 15th amendments provided a solid foundation for urban blacks wishing to exercise their citizenship rights. It was here that the first organizations were formed to campaign for civil rights. In 1905, W. E. B. Du Bois (1868-1963), a Northern academic, founded the short-lived Niagara Movement to attack Washington's position and campaign for 'full manhood rights' for all black people. In 1909, the bi-racial National Association for the Advancement of Coloured People (NAACP) was formed, with Du Bois as director of publicity. Its aim was 'to achieve … equal citizenship rights for all … by eliminating segregation and discrimination'. Its secret weapon was its collection of lawyers, who would challenge segregation in the courts through a series of assaults on the Plessy ruling.

W. E. B. Du Bois.

Twentieth-century America

Economic depression, crop disease, racial violence and wartime demands drove more than 1 million blacks to move north between 1919 and 1925 to find work in large industrial cities. Over the next 50 years, the proportion of blacks in the South dropped from 90 to 50 per cent. Racial resentment in the North (as whites found themselves competing for work and housing),

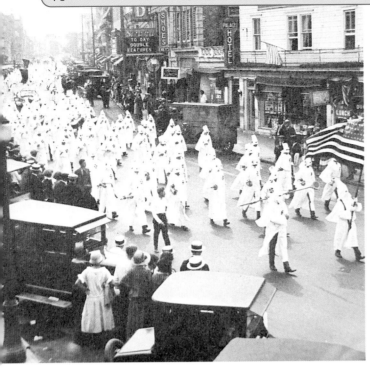

The Klu Klux Klan parade through a Southern town, 1925.

encouraged by a revived KKK, led to the 'red summer' of 1919. Twenty-five major race riots erupted across the USA in a taste of things to come.

During the Second World War (1939-45), the NAACP was transformed into a mass organization by the subscriptions of thousands of black servicemen who were infuriated by unequal treatment in the armed services. Although black and white soldiers fought together for the first time in 1945, military segregation was not abolished until 1948. While the NAACP concentrated on bringing lawsuits, a different type of organization was founded in 1942. The Congress of Racial Equality (CORE) would use non-violent direct action to achieve change.

1948: A. Philip Randolph (left) leads a protest against segregation in the army.

A. Philip Randolph (1889-1979), a black labour leader, won the first major victory for civil rights in 1941. By threatening a mass march on Washington DC, which would have caused international embarrassment, he forced President Franklin Roosevelt to issue a special Executive Order banning racial discrimination in the booming defence industries.

During the 1930s and 1940s, a series of successful lawsuits brought by the NAACP forced many school districts to improve their black schools. Then, on 17 May 1954, the Brown v. Board of Education of Topeka Supreme Court ruling rejected the 'separate but equal' doctrine and outlawed segregation in schools, opening the floodgates for further legal challenges. The South responded by setting up local Citizens' Councils (made up of business and professional people) to fight its implementation. The fight for rights was on.

The murder of Emmett Till

The Brown decision provided a legal basis for challenging segregation, but another event had a more emotional effect on support for the civil rights movement: the lynching of Emmet Till, a 14-year-old boy from Chicago, visiting relatives in Money, Mississippi.

On 28 August, Till was kidnapped in the middle of the night and beaten to death by two men. His crime? Saying 'Bye, Baby!' and wolf-whistling at the white woman who ran the town store. When Till's body was returned to Chicago for burial, it was almost unrecognizable – the head was crushed in on one side, one eye was gouged out and a bullet was lodged in the skull. His grief-stricken mother held an open-coffin funeral to show the nation what had been done to her son. Horrified whites responded by pouring money into the NAACP war chest.

Till's killers were arrested and found not guilty by an all-white jury, despite eyewitness testimony. After the trial, the black witnesses had to be moved out of the state for their own protection. The anger and grief provoked by Till's murder aroused a determination to change things for the better. As one civil rights leader commented, 'it just set in concrete the determination of the people to move forward.'

Post-war momentum

'I think the beginning of this period from 1954 has its roots in the returning soldiers after 1945 … There was a building up of militancy, not so much by going into the streets as by a feeling of "We're not going to put up with this anymore." … What made 1954 so unusual was that the … Brown decision established black people as being citizens with the rights of all other citizens. Once that happened, then it was very easy for the militancy … to express itself …'
(Bayard Rustin, quoted in Hampton and Fayer, *Voices of Freedom*)

Coming of age in Mississippi

Anne Moody was 14 at the time of Till's murder. Her mother urged her to avoid trouble by pretending not to have heard about it. But this reaction had as great an impact on Anne as the murder itself:

'I was fifteen years old when I began to hate white people. I hated … all the other whites who were responsible for countless murders … I also hated Negroes. I hated them for not standing up and doing something about the murders …'
(Moody, *Coming of Age in Mississippi*)

PROTEST MOVEMENTS 1955–62

The Montgomery bus boycott (1955-56)

In the Southern states, segregation on public transport gave blacks a daily reminder of their inferior status. Having paid their fares at the front of the bus, they had to re-enter by the rear door and sit in a blacks-only section at the back. If a white passenger was left standing, a whole row of blacks had to give up their seats, as blacks were forbidden to sit next to whites.

Rosa Parks with her lawyer, Charles D. Langford, 1956.

On 1 December 1955, Rosa Parks, a seamstress from Montgomery, Alabama, took her usual bus home. When the driver noticed a white man standing, he demanded that her row give up their seats. Parks refused to move. She was reported to the police and arrested for violating the city's 'whites first' bus laws.

Parks was the first 'respectable' person to defy the bus laws, so E. D. Nixon, a NAACP activist, decided to use her case to fight the segregation laws. With local church ministers, he founded the Montgomery Improvement Association (MIA), with 26-year-old Martin Luther King as president. The MIA reinforced its legal case with grassroots action. Thousands of leaflets were distributed urging people to stop using the buses on the day of Parks' trial. When this proved successful, an MIA meeting voted to extend the protest indefinitely. It lasted 13 months.

The events in Montgomery attracted the attention of Bayard Rustin, a veteran pacifist and campaigner. He advised the MIA on tactics and introduced King to Mohandas ('Mahatma') Gandhi's non-violent direct action. It was the first time civil rights activists from North and South had worked together.

Why I walked

Gussie Nesbitt, a 53-year-old domestic worker and NAACP member, was typical of the 40,000 boycotters who refused to ride the buses:

'Before the boycott, we were stuffed in the back of the bus just like cattle … if you sat down on the bus, the bus driver would say, "Let me have that seat, nigger". And you'd have to get up … That's how it was and that's why I walked. I wanted to be one of them that tried to make it better. I didn't want somebody else to make it better for me.'
(Quoted in Hampton and Fayer, *Voices of Freedom*)

As tensions escalated, white extremists firebombed King's and Nixon's homes. King's powerful rhetoric ensured that the black community did not respond in kind. In February, 89 people were arrested under an obscure anti-boycott law, but the tactic backfired after media coverage of their trial transformed a local boycott into a national story.

On 20 December, the Supreme Court confirmed that Alabama's bus segregation laws were unconstitutional, following the precedent set by the 1954 Brown ruling. In January 1957, Rustin persuaded black church leaders to build on their victory by founding the Southern Christian Leadership Conference (SCLC) to co-ordinate their future efforts. With King as its president, it soon became a leading force in the civil rights movement.

The Montgomery boycott's success showed blacks what could be accomplished with non-violent protest, but the momentum for change stalled when local boycotts failed to take off across the South. It took a radical initiative from the younger generation to kickstart the process.

Martin Luther King, March 1956.

Sitting in at a lunch counter in Nashville, February 1960.

The sit-in movement (1960)

On 1 February 1960, four black students walked into a Woolworth's store in Greensboro, North Carolina, sat down at the whites-only lunch counter and ordered coffee. They were refused service but remained there until the store closed. Each day they returned with more volunteers. By the end of the week over 400 students (black and white) were sitting in shifts at the lunch counter. News of their action spurred other students and sit-ins soon spread to over 100 southern cities.

Previous one-off sit-ins had failed to attract media attention. But many young activists, impatient with the slow pace of desegregation, were ready for action. In non-violence workshops, James Lawson, an ex-missionary based in Nashville, used the tactics of passive resistance to teach students how to sit peacefully while being verbally and physically abused. In

Cleansing the soul

Franklin McCain, one of the Greensboro four, recalled how he felt after taking part in the original sit-in:

'If it's possible to know what it means to have your soul cleansed – I felt pretty clean at that time. I probably felt better on that day than I've ever felt in my life. Seems like a lot of feelings of guilt or what-have-you suddenly left me, and I felt as though I had gained my manhood ....'
(Quoted in Cook, *Sweet Land of Liberty*)

A holy crusade

John Lewis, a 20-year-old Lawson-trained activist, recalled what
happened during the second week of a sit-in at Woolworth's lunch
counter in Nashville:

'A group of young white men came and they started pulling and beating
primarily the young women. They put lighted cigarettes down their backs,
in their hair, and they were really beating people. In a short time police
officials came in and placed all of us under arrest, and not a single member
of the white group, the people that were opposing our sit-in, was arrested
… To go to jail was to bring shame and disgrace on the family. But for me,
it was like being involved in a holy crusade, it became a badge of honour.'
(Quoted in Hampton and Fayer, *Voices of Freedom*)

some states, protestors found it easy
to integrate the lunch counters, but
in others they were kicked, beaten
and sprayed with food.

In April, the students formed the
Student Non-violent Co-ordinating
Committee (SNCC), signalling a
major shift in the civil rights
movement's support. Younger
activists were more militant and
were not affected by the threat of
economic reprisals.

Within a year, 70,000 people had
taken part in mass sit-ins and 4,000
had been arrested, transforming the
struggle for civil rights into a

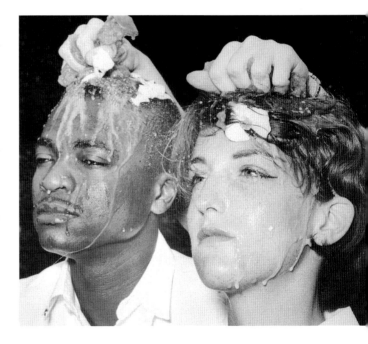

Two trainees practise
passive resistance, as eggs
are broken over their heads.

genuine social movement. But differences in strategy marked
the beginnings of a rift within the movement. CORE was
transformed from a small group of pacifists into an effective
civil rights organization, while the more conservative NAACP
unwillingly surrendered its leadership to people who were
prepared to take their protests into the streets.

President John F. Kennedy at his inauguration (left), with Vice President Lyndon B. Johnson, January 1961.

The freedom rides (1961)

John F. Kennedy was sworn in as US president in 1961. His dependence on Southern support meant that civil rights were low on his list of priorities. In May 1961, the 'freedom rides' marked Kennedy's first big civil rights test.

Inspired by the sit-in movement and encouraged by a recent Supreme Court ruling banning segregation in interstate transport terminals, CORE sent a bi-racial group of 13 volunteers on a freedom ride from Washington DC to New Orleans. CORE's leader, James Farmer, had a clear strategy. He understood that the government would not enforce federal law unless it had to, fearing reprisals from Southern politicians. So he made it harder for the government to do nothing by provoking a violent reaction. Black freedom riders sat at the front of the bus, and at every rest stop they used the facilities reserved for whites; white freedom riders did the reverse.

James Farmer, leader of CORE, August 1964.

On reaching Alabama, one bus was surrounded by a KKK mob outside Anniston and firebombed; another was attacked in Birmingham and the riders beaten senseless. Spurred on by media coverage of these violent incidents, Nashville students volunteered to continue the freedom ride.

Further violence in Montgomery was shown on national television. Reluctantly forced to act, Kennedy sent in federal marshals to restore order. In Jackson, Mississippi, the riders were arrested and thrown in jail.

Throughout the summer, thousands of black and white activists travelled on buses across the South, filling up the jails. In September, the Interstate Commerce

Bloodied but unbowed

When the freedom riders reached Montgomery, James Zwerg, a white student, was savagely beaten and another rider was left paralysed. Fellow rider Fred Leonard recalled what happened:

'And then, all of a sudden ... White people, sticks and bricks. "Niggers! Kill the Niggers!" We were still on the bus. I think we were all thinking maybe we should go off at the back of this bus ... But we decided no, no, we'll go off the front and take what's coming to us ... Jim Zwerg ... he had a lot of nerve. I think that's what saved [us] ... 'cause [he] walked off the bus in front of us and it was like the people in the mob were possessed. They couldn't believe there was a white man who would help us, and they grabbed him and pulled him into the mob. When we came off the bus, their attention was on him. It was like they didn't see the rest of us...'
(Quoted in Hampton and Fayer, *Voices of Freedom*)

Commission (ICC) prohibited the use of segregated facilities by interstate bus companies. Obeying these regulations now became a state rather than federal responsibility.

The success of the freedom rides inspired many students to leave college and become full-time organizers in the South. However, success was soon followed by failure in the SCLC's first major campaign against segregation.

May 1961: two freedom riders take part in a march outside the Trailways Bus Terminal in New York. James Peck (right) received the injury to his head three days earlier, when a bus of freedom riders was attacked in Birmingham, Alabama.

Martin Luther King leads a line of protestors along a street in Albany, December 1961.

Albany (1961-62)

In November 1961, students from Albany, Georgia, led by two SNCC activists, were arrested and jailed for 'testing' the ICC ruling. In response, the Albany Movement (AM) was founded to co-ordinate the various civic groups' demands for desegregation. A month later the arrest of nine freedom riders brought Albany's black community onto the streets and hundreds were arrested. The AM invited King to Albany to assist their campaign and ensure media coverage. On 16 December, he led 250 marchers to the city hall, where they were arrested for parading without a permit. Albany's police chief, Laurie Pritchett, had learned the lesson of previous clashes in Alabama – that violence attracted bad publicity and federal intervention. He banned the use of clubs or dogs, ordering his officers to arrest protestors with minimum force.

King vowed to stay in jail until the city was desegregated. However, the city commissioners negotiated an agreement with rival AM leaders that they would stop the demonstrations in return for the desegregation of the bus terminal and talks on segregation policies. Thinking his work was done, King left town, but the commissioners broke their promises and the AM broke down into factional bickering.

Seven months later, when King returned to receive his delayed sentence, he chose to go to jail rather than admit guilt by paying a fine. Again he was released unwillingly, after the cunning Pritchett arranged for his fine to be paid. Media interest then fizzled out, and when the city obtained a federal court order preventing further demonstrations, King reluctantly obeyed. Local support dwindled and the more militant SNCC members openly criticized his tactics.

In August, black frustrations turned to violence when a policeman savagely beat up a pregnant woman. 'Did you see them non-violent rocks?', Pritchett asked reporters. King was furious and the movement appeared to be collapsing. When the Attorney General refused to intervene, King returned to Atlanta. After months of protest, nothing had been achieved.

This was the civil rights movement's first major setback. Outmanoeuvred by police and city authorities, ignored by the Kennedy administration and weakened by disunity within the AM, King was blamed for its failure. With these lessons behind him, he resolved that the next confrontation would be on his own terms.

A great big hoax

After King had left Albany, the city officials refused to negotiate any further on desegregation. Deeply embarrassed, King later told reporters:

'I'm sorry I was bailed out. I didn't understand at the time what was happening. We thought that the victory had been won. When we got out we discovered it was all a hoax.' (Quoted in Oates, *Let the Trumpet Sound*)

December 1961: police chief Laurie Pritchett tells Martin Luther King and Dr W. G. Anderson that they are under arrest, after they could not produce a permit to parade.

I HAVE A DREAM

Birmingham, Alabama (1963)

In April 1963, the Reverend Shuttlesworth, a dedicated campaigner, asked the SCLC to choose Birmingham, Alabama's largest, most segregated city, as the target for its next campaign. Birmingham was controlled by the state's new governor, George Wallace, whose election slogan was: 'Segregation now, segregation tomorrow, segregation forever!'

Code-named 'Project C' (for 'confrontation'), the campaign's aim was more focused than in Albany, demanding the desegregation of all department stores and an end to employment discrimination. The campaign almost collapsed after a week through a lack of volunteers willing to be arrested and because of light-handed policing by Birmingham's notorious police chief, 'Bull' Connor. With only 150 arrests and no violence, the media were losing interest. So King raised the stakes by defying a court order and getting arrested himself.

In jail, he wrote his famous 'Letter from a Birmingham Jail', explaining why civil disobedience was necessary to achieve

The Children's Crusade

The Reverend James Bevel, a veteran of the Nashville sit-ins and one of King's lieutenants in Birmingham, thought up the Children's Crusade. He recalled the thinking behind getting younger people involved:

'So the strategy was, okay, let's use thousands of people who won't create an economic crisis because they're off the job: the high school students … A boy from high school, he can get the same effect in terms of being in jail, in terms of putting the pressure on the city, as his father – and yet there is no economic threat on the family because the father is still on the job.'
(Quoted in Hampton and Fayer, *Voices of Freedom*)

essential change. He concluded: 'Freedom is never voluntarily given by the oppressor; it must be demanded by the oppressed.'

A month later the campaign was again in danger of collapsing, but it was saved by two events: the 'Children's Crusade' and Connor's decision to take a more hardline approach. Most of the people arrested so far had been middle-class adults. But now SCLC organizers started recruiting thousands of high-school students. On 2 May, over 600 students (some as young as six) were arrested as they marched out of Birmingham's churches singing 'We shall overcome'. Many more marchers soon hit the streets. On the second day Connor's restraint collapsed, and he ordered the firemen to turn their high-powered hoses on the marchers. Jets of water blasted children and spectators to the ground. When angry spectators pelted the police with stones, snarling dogs were released.

Police chief 'Bull' Connor, May 1963.

Young marchers try to stand up to the power of the hoses.

Televised scenes of women and children being hosed, clubbed and attacked by dogs shocked the nation. Fearing a racial explosion, President Kennedy sent his best negotiator to force a settlement with the city council. Once again, the tactics of non-violent confrontation had brought moral victory to the civil rights movement.

King called off the protests just in time. A day later, two KKK firebombs on SCLC buildings and police handling of the angry crowds triggered off serious riots, providing a taster of what lay ahead. Federal troops were called in to restore peace.

Victory in Birmingham had an electrifying effect on blacks throughout the South. Caught up by the new mood of defiance, they poured onto the streets of over 100 cities demanding their basic rights. By the end of the summer, 15,000 people had been arrested in the biggest wave of black militancy ever witnessed in the USA.

On 11 June, Kennedy told the nation, 'We face a moral crisis as a country and a people … it is time to act. The events in Birmingham and elsewhere have so impressed the desire for equality that no city or state can choose to ignore them.' Recognizing that civil rights crises could no longer be solved one at a time, he bowed to demands for new legislation and presented a wide-ranging Civil Rights bill to Congress.

June 1963: blacks throw rocks and bottles at police in Jackson, Mississippi.

March on Washington

Many blacks found little to celebrate on the 100th anniversary of Lincoln's Emancipation Proclamation in 1963. They were twice as likely to be unemployed, their incomes were half those of whites and less than 10 per cent of Southern black students were attending integrated schools, despite the Supreme Court ruling.

A. Philip Randolph and Bayard Rustin wanted to commemorate the centenary by organizing a huge bi-racial march to Washington to demand more job opportunities for blacks and show public support for the new Civil Rights bill. On 28 August, over 200,000 marchers gathered at the Lincoln Memorial in Washington DC in the largest protest demonstration in American history.

King made the most important speech of his life that day – a message of hope and determination. His appeal to whites to support the civil rights crusade and his vision of an integrated future delighted the crowd. King's popularity stemmed from his ability to express the ideals of racial equality and to provide black Americans with a powerful collective voice. His position

King addresses the crowd in Washington: 'I have a dream'.

I have a dream

At the end of his speech King spoke without notes:

'I have a dream that one day this nation will rise up and live out the true meaning of its creed, "We hold these truths to be self-evident, that all men are created equal." I have a dream that one day on the red hills of Georgia, sons of former slaves and sons of former slaveholders will be able to sit down together at the table of brotherhood … I have a dream that my four little children will one day live in a nation where they will not be judged by the colour of their skin, but by the content of their character … and when we allow freedom to ring … from every village and every hamlet … we will be able to speed up the day when all God's children … will be able to join hands and sing in the words of the old Negro spiritual: "Free at last. Free at last. Thank God almighty, we are free at last".'
(Quoted in Oates, *Let the Trumpet Sound*)

Participants in the march on Washington jam the area in front of the Lincoln Memorial and on either side of the Reflecting Pool.

at the centre of the civil rights coalition was a focus of unity for the disparate groups. For a brief moment King's vision gripped the USA, and he was named *Time* magazine's Man of the Year. His moderate leadership was also admired outside the USA, and he was awarded the Nobel Peace Prize in October 1964 for 'keeping his followers to the principle of non-violence'.

A spiritual experience

William H. Johnson, a Second World War veteran and New York City policeman, travelled to Washington to provide security for the march:

'I was enthralled by Dr King's Speech. Oh my God, it just seemed to move you almost off the platform, off the earth. A big 'ole ox like me, it made my eyes water a little bit ... it was a matter of being inspired and moved ... [a] spiritual experience.'
(Quoted in Hampton and Fayer, *Voices of Freedom*)

Two weeks after King's 'dream' speech, an explosion at the Sixteenth Street Baptist church in Birmingham killed four black girls and injured 21. Young blacks responded with violence, and in ensuing riots two more were killed and several businesses burned down.

After President Kennedy's assassination in November 1963, his successor, President Lyndon Johnson, succeeded in passing the Civil Rights bill through Congress in July 1964. The Civil Rights Act banned segregation in public places, forbade discrimination in government-funded programmes and established an Equal Opportunity Commission. Although it marked the end of Jim Crow, it failed to guarantee voting rights for all blacks. This became the civil rights movement's last major campaign.

THE RIGHT TO VOTE

Mississippi was the poorest American state and at the heart of Southern resistance to demands for the right to vote. The power of the black vote had become evident during the Reconstruction, when Ulysses Grant won the 1868 presidential election by 307,000 votes (with over 450,000 black votes).

Outnumbered whites (in some areas blacks made up 80 per cent of the population) were determined to cling to power, and blacks who tried to register to vote could expect retaliation from the police, the Citizens' Councils or the KKK. They might lose their job, their home or even their life, like Reverend George Lee, who was shot in the face in 1955 while leading a voter registration campaign in his county.

Intimidation meant that less than 5 per cent of Mississippi blacks were registered. Having failed to find a legal solution,

Ulysses Simpson Grant was elected president of the USA in 1868. His majority was only 307,000 out of a total of 5.7 million votes. Nearly all the 500,000 black voters voted for him.

The proportion of non-whites in the states, in the late twentieth century.

Percentage of non-whites in the population
- under 10
- 10-20
- 20-30
- 30-40

NAACP and SNCC organizers started working on a voter registration programme in 1961. Fear was pervasive. Many of the students attending the first demonstrations were ostracized by their families, who were afraid of what white people might do to them.

In 1962, the SNCC, CORE, NAACP and SCLC pooled their resources and formed the Council of Federated Organizations (COFO). Federal funds were used to set up the Voter Education Project (VEP) in the South. The government hoped this would steer the civil rights movement towards less confrontational activities, but if anything there was more violence. COFO workers were regularly shot at, intimidated and arrested; the NAACP's main organizer in Mississippi, Medgar Evers, was killed. His killer was later acquitted.

COFO held a mock election (the 'Freedom Vote') in summer 1963, and over 90,000 blacks practised casting their votes. Having confronted the fear and proved black political apathy to be a myth, COFO resolved to organize a much larger campaign the following summer.

Mississippi Freedom Summer and the MFDP

In 1964, COFO established the 'Freedom Summer' project in Mississippi. It had four main goals: registering local blacks to

Dealing with fear

The courage of COFO workers was a major factor in persuading Southern blacks to register as voters. Ivanhoe Donaldson recalled how volunteers learned to deal with fear:

'You learned how to live with it, how to function with it. Almost every organiser in the Deep South was constantly faced with harassment. They'd been beaten, they'd been shot at … If you showed fear, it affected the community around you, so you had to show this was just a regular part of life. And people, if they saw you had confidence, developed confidence.'
(Quoted in Hampton and Fayer, *Voices of Freedom*)

A racist objective?

Mississippi's white community prepared itself for the 'invasion' of civil rights workers by doubling its police force and stockpiling extra arms. William Simpson, a spokesman for the White Citizens' Councils in Mississippi, explained their opposition:

'Black people have had voting rights in this state all along ... The objective of this student invasion was to eliminate all the qualifications, to have mass voting and frankly, to advance black political power. They were asked to vote not as American citizens, but to vote as blacks. It was a very racist objective. As such, it was opposed ... to say they were not warmly welcomed and received is perhaps an understatement.' (Quoted in Hampton and Fayer, *Voices of Freedom*)

vote; organizing an integrated branch of the Democratic Party; setting up freedom schools; and setting up community centres.

Local leaders invited Northern white students to help with the campaign. For maximum impact, they concentrated on voter registration in counties with majority black populations and active White Citizens' Councils. The Mississippi governor

Marchers on the 1966 'March against Fear' show their solidarity with Mississippi farm labourers, to encourage them to vote.

declared the project an invasion and promised resistance. In June, three civil rights workers (two of them white) disappeared, sparking off a federal investigation. During the summer, 60 black churches and houses were burned, five civil rights workers murdered, 80 injured and hundreds arrested.

Fannie Lou Hamer, 1964.

The Mississippi Freedom Democratic Party (MFDP) was established to publicize the exclusion of blacks from the political process. Fannie Lou Hamer, the MFDP's vice-chairman, was a sharecropper who had lost her job and home in 1962 for daring to register. The embodiment of grassroots leadership in action, she inspired thousands to follow her example.

In August, an MFDP delegation attempted to replace the official whites-only Mississippi delegation at the Democratic Party's National Convention. It failed, having rejected a compromise banning future segregated delegations and allowing MFDP delegates to attend as spectators. The delegates returned home disillusioned with politics, unwilling to betray their 90,000 Mississippi supporters.

These events exposed again the divisions between the older, more pragmatic SCLC/NAACP and the younger, more radical SNCC/CORE. This, along with growing black assertiveness, would influence subsequent movements (such as Black Power) seeking a more radical transformation of American society.

Selma, Alabama (1965)

Since 1963, blacks in Selma, Alabama, and nearby Marion had repeatedly attempted to register as voters at the county courthouse, only to be turned back by police or arrested. Frustrated by their lack of progress, local leaders invited the SCLC to step in and raise the profile of their campaign.

King held a series of demonstrations outside the county courthouse. By the end of January 1965 over 2,000 blacks had been arrested, but police restraint meant there was little media interest. Once again, it was the spectacle of violence that brought the required response. On 26 February, Jimmie Jackson, a demonstrator on a night march in Marion, was shot and beaten to death by state troopers. Jackson's death proved a severe test of patience for King's followers. So he immediately announced a march from Selma to Montgomery (the state capital) to focus their anger and increase their media profile. Governor Wallace responded by prohibiting the march.

Dispersing demonstrators in Montgomery, March 1965.

On 7 March, six hundred demonstrators left Selma and found their route barred by state troopers. Ordered to disperse, the marchers kneeled to pray. Before rolling news cameras, troopers and police rode their horses straight into the crowd, whipping and clubbing the protestors. Over fifty people were seriously injured and the march was forced to turn back.

President Johnson condemned the violence and thousands of

Running for my life

Eight-year-old Sheyann Webb recalled what happened on Sunday 7 March when the demonstrators reached Pettus Bridge just outside Selma:

'As we approached the bridge, I was getting more and more frightened … I could see hundreds of policemen, state troopers, billy clubs, dogs and horses, and I began to just cry. I remember the ministers who were at the front of the line saying, "Kneel down to pray" … all I could remember was outbursts of tear gas and I saw people being beaten and I began to run home as fast as I could … People were running and falling … you'd hear people scream and hear the whips swishing and you'd hear them striking people … And I ran and I ran and I ran. It was like I was running for my life.'
(Quoted in Wexler, *The Civil Rights Movement: An Eyewitness History*)

people attended sympathy demonstrations. King asked supporters to gather for a second march on 9 June and many Northern sympathizers travelled to Selma. Wishing to avoid further violence, King struck a secret deal with the government to turn back at an agreed point. He led 1,500 marchers out of town and back again, causing much confusion and disappointment. The so-called 'Tuesday turnaround' pushed the underlying tensions between the SNCC and SCLC to breaking point and many SNCC workers abandoned the Selma campaign in disgust.

That evening a white clergyman from Boston was beaten to death by whites. The national outcry that followed – contrasting with the official silence that accompanied Jackson's death – was the last straw. Four days later, Johnson delivered a new Voting Rights bill to Congress and praised the courage of the demonstrators: 'It is not just Negroes but all of us who must overcome the crippling legacy of bigotry and injustice. And we shall overcome.' This identification with the movement's slogan showed the white resistance that the president meant business.

Martin Luther King and his wife Coretta lead thousands of demonstrators on the final part of the march from Selma to Montgomery.

On 21 March 1965, the Selma to Montgomery march resumed with federal protection. On reaching Montgomery four days later, King told a 25,000-strong rally: 'We are on the move now. Like an idea whose time has come, not even the marching of mighty armies can halt us. We are moving to the land of freedom.' Four months later, Johnson signed the Voting Rights Act, extending federal powers to abolish all the technical tricks (such as literacy tests) that had been used to prevent blacks from voting. Within a year, 430,000 new black voters had been registered in the 11 Southern states, and within five years the number of elected black officials had grown from 200 to 1,500.

BLACK SEPARATISM

Marcus Garvey

Apart from the bi-racial NAACP, there was no real alternative black organization until the arrival of Marcus Garvey (1887-1940), a Jamaican immigrant and founder of the Universal Negro Improvement Association (UNIA), in 1916. Garvey was the first to promote black separatism, calling for blacks to live apart from whites and regard Africa as their true homeland.

Garvey set up branches of the UNIA in all the major Northern cities, winning the support of thousands of urban blacks, who were dissatisfied with the gradual reformism offered by the NAACP. Preaching a mixture of black pride (he coined the phrase, 'Black is Beautiful') and economic self-sufficiency, Garvey argued that black people should create their own society. To help achieve this he organized a 'Back to Africa'

Marcus Garvey (in plumed hat and uniform) drives through Harlem, New York City, in 1924.

Up, up you mighty race

Garvey often started his speeches with a rousing call to arms and intoxicating vision of bringing the scattered children of Africa together into one mighty force:

'Up, up you mighty race! You can accomplish what you will! ... Every American Negro and every West Indian Negro must understand that there is but one fatherland for the Negro, and that is Africa ... We say to the white man who now dominates Africa, that it is in his interest to clear out of Africa now, because we are coming ... and we mean to retake every square inch of ... African territory that belongs to us by right Divine.' (Quoted in Carson, *The Eyes on the Prize: A Civil Rights Reader*)

movement, creating the Black Star Line to ship black Americans to Liberia, a West African state created in 1822 for ex-slaves.

However, Garvey's teachings antagonized many within the black establishment who supported interracial co-operation. When he joined forces with the KKK in 1922, to help promote his policy of racial exclusion, Du Bois called him 'the most dangerous enemy of the Negro race in America and the world'. In 1923, Garvey was arrested for fraud over the Black Star Line and deported to Jamaica.

Garvey was the first black leader to build up a mass organization. By 1925, the UNIA had over one million members (dwarfing the NAACP). His teachings inspired black nationalist leaders like Malcolm X and Stokely Carmichael.

Malcolm X and the Nation of Islam

Garvey's separatist message was taken up by the Nation of Islam (NOI), a religious organization founded in Detroit in 1930. Its leader, Elijah Muhammad, claimed to be a prophet of Allah. He taught that black people were Allah's original creation and all other races were the result of a mad black scientist's genetic experiments. The whites ('blue-eyed devils') were the worst and had become the blacks' natural enemy after toppling them from their position as rulers of the world. NOI followers believed that whites would eventually be destroyed and blacks would reclaim their rightful place.

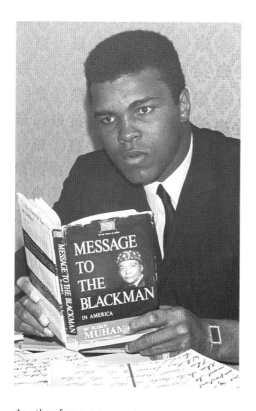

Another famous supporter of the Nation of Islam was the boxer Muhammad Ali (formerly Cassius Clay), seen here reading a book by the NOI leader, Elijah Muhammad.

The NOI's most famous spokesman was Malcolm X (1925-65). His real name was Little, which he changed to 'X' (representing his unknown African family name taken from his slave ancestors) after converting to the NOI while in prison. On his release, Malcolm preached the NOI gospel of racial separatism and religious fundamentalism and soon became one of the NOI's most effective speakers. By 1960, the movement's membership had risen to 100,000.

Malcolm X addresses an audience of students in London, UK, 1965.

As a Temple minister in Harlem, New York, Malcolm gained a dedicated following through a mixture of angry rhetoric and biting humour. He often compared the effects of racial integration to diluting black coffee with cream, 'It used to be strong, it becomes weak. It used to wake you up, now it puts you to sleep.'

Multiple voices, multiple strategies

Marian Wright recalled the effect of hearing Malcolm X speak for the first time when a student at Yale Law School in the early 1960s:

'He expressed the rage that all of us continued to feel about the slow pace of change in the country, but he did it in the cleverest and funniest way you could imagine … he was blunt where King was tactful … He could say the anger … Malcolm was a reinforcing person and responded to a different need in us … Even though we believed in non-violence, it was also very good to have somebody vent the other side. There always need to be multiple voices with multiple strategies pursuing social change.'
(Quoted in Hampton and Fayer, *Voices of Freedom*)

Malcolm and King represented opposing views: Malcolm preached racial separatism and 'complete equality by any means necessary'; King preached racial tolerance and non-violence. But although he often criticized the methods of the civil rights movement, Malcolm respected the courage of King and the SNCC students.

In June 1964, disillusioned by Muhammad's personal behaviour, Malcolm left the NOI and formed his own group, the Organization of Afro-American Unity (OAAU). After returning from a pilgrimage to Mecca, where he had seen Muslims of all colours united by their common beliefs, he abandoned separatism in favour of a more conciliatory approach.

Joining the civil rights bandwagon, Malcolm developed an effective tactic of presenting himself as the violent alternative to King's moderation. After King and other demonstrators were imprisoned in Selma in 1965, Malcolm told a mass rally: 'I don't advocate violence, but if a man steps on my toes, I'll step on his … whites better be glad Martin Luther King is rallying the people, because other forces are waiting to take over if he fails!'

Growing hostility between Malcolm and rivals from the NOI led to many threats against his life. In February 1965, he was

Malcolm was our manhood

At Malcolm X's funeral, an actor, Ossie Davies, gave a moving eulogy, summing up Malcolm's importance to his supporters:

'Many will … say he's … a fanatic, a racist … And we will answer and say unto them, Did you ever talk to Brother Malcolm? … Did you ever really listen to him? … Was he himself ever associated with violence or any public disturbance? … if you knew him, you would know why we must honour him: Malcolm was our manhood, our living black manhood! And in honouring him, we honour the best in ourselves.'
(Quoted in Hampton and Fayer, *Voices of Freedom*)

shot dead at a rally in Harlem. Three black Muslims were convicted of his murder.

Throughout his adult life, the press portrayed Malcolm as a hate-mongering racist. But his main message was to urge blacks to close ranks and unite, before integrating with white society from a position of strength. By highlighting the limitations of the civil rights movement, especially its failure to address the economic deprivation of the Northern black ghettos, he pushed King towards a more radical and wide-ranging agenda. After his death, Malcolm became an icon for young urban blacks and inspired the emerging Black Power movement of the late 1960s.

Stokely Carmichael, 1967.

The rise of Black Power

After the sit-ins of 1961, many SNCC workers moved to rural communities where they played a vital role in the civil rights movement, starting grassroots programmes and encouraging local organizers. In March 1965, John Hulett, a local activist, invited Stokely Carmichael (1941-98), an experienced SNCC activist from the Mississippi Freedom Summer movement, to Lowndes County, Alabama, to promote voter registration.

Inspired by Malcolm X and the MFDP, Carmichael founded the first black political party, the Lowndes County Freedom Organization (LCFO), with Hulett as chairman. They chose a snarling black panther for their symbol, because 'he never bothers anything, but when you start pushing him, he moves backwards, backwards and backwards in his corner, and then he comes out to destroy what's before him'. On election day, intimidation ensured that the LCFO received less than 50 per cent of the vote and all seven candidates were defeated. However, it provided the inspiration for the Black Panther Party, founded almost a year later.

In 1966, both the SNCC and CORE elected militant leaders. When Carmichael became chair of the SNCC, it changed its official policy from integration to separatism, expelling all whites from its organization (CORE followed a year later). Many of the SNCC's new supporters were attracted by its militant politics rather than its Southern projects. As a result, many of its best programmes died from lack of support and the loss of vital funds from white supporters.

The divisions between the radical SNCC/CORE and more conservative SCLC/NAACP were highlighted in June 1966 during James Meredith's Mississippi 'March against Fear'.

Dick Gregory, Martin Luther King and James Meredith, on the 'March against Fear'.

Whites and civil rights

Soon after Carmichael was elected chairman of the SNCC he published an essay, 'What We Want', in which he explained that whites could still play a role from outside the civil rights movement:

'... most liberal whites react to Black Power, with the question, "What about me?", rather than saying: "Tell me what you want me to do and I'll see if I can do it ..." One of the most disturbing things about almost all white supporters of the movement has been that they are afraid to go into their own communities – which is where the racism exists – and work to get rid of it ... let them preach nonviolence in the white community.'
(Quoted in the *New York Review of Books*, 22 September 1966)

(Meredith was the first black student to enter the University of Mississippi in 1962, setting off a major riot that ended with two deaths.) When Meredith was shot and wounded three days into his march, leaders from all groups (except the NAACP) vowed to continue. It would be the last great march of the civil rights movement before it split apart.

During this march Carmichael first used the slogan 'Black Power!' Many of the marchers immediately rallied to it, dropping the SCLC's chant of 'Freedom Now!' The media seized on Black Power as a sign of divisions within the movement over integration versus separatism.

The movement came to international attention during the 1968 Mexico Olympic games, when two black athletes used the Black Power salute (raising a clenched fist) to protest against racial conditions in the USA. Soon Black Power was being interpreted in different ways: militant groups saw it as a call to self-defence; others took a cultural approach, stressing their African roots through a revival of interest in black history and African names, hairstyles and fashions.

Anti-Negro

Black Power was condemned by many of the older black leaders, including Bayard Rustin, a founder member of the SCLC, who argued that:

'Black power not only lacks any real value for the civil rights movement, but … its [growth] is positively harmful. It diverts the movement from a meaningful debate over strategy and tactics, it isolates the Negro community and it encourages the growth of anti-Negro forces.'
(Quoted in Johnson, *Stokely Carmichael: The Story of Black Power*)

Tommie Smith and John Carlos, gold and bronze medal winners of the men's 200 metres at the 1968 Olympics, give the Black Power salute. Afterwards they were banned from the US athletics team.

Huey Newton (right) and
Bobby Seale, founders of
the Black Panthers.

The Black Panther Party

The most radical Black Power group was the Black Panther
Party for Self-Defense (BPP). Founded in Oakland, California,
in October 1966 by Huey Newton and Bobby Seale, its aim
was twofold: to confront police brutality; and to support the
black community through practical welfare programmes, such
as health clinics and free school breakfasts.

Black Panther poster of the
1960s.

Borrowing its name and emblem from the
LCFO and ideas from Malcolm X and
Marxism, the BPP incorporated its main
demands into a 10-point manifesto. These
included equal opportunities in employment
and housing, exemption from military
service, black juries, an end to 'police
brutality and murder' and an independent
black state in the USA. Although the BPP's
membership peaked at only 5,000, it had
strong support in the ghetto communities of
large American cities.

The BPP's early activities focused on
monitoring police behaviour – armed patrols
followed the police about the ghetto and
advised 'suspects' of their legal rights. It soon
gained media attention, more for its striking
'uniform' (black beret, trousers and leather

A new kind of organization

Emory Douglas, an illustrator and painter from Harlem, recalled his parents' attitudes to him after he joined the Black Panthers in 1967:

'My parents, my neighbours, were ... kind of standoffish in their attitudes towards the Black Panther party, because here you had a new, dynamic kind of organization coming out and doing things that never had been done in the history of this country before – carrying guns, standing up to the police, standing up to the power structure, demanding the rights that we were supposed to have.'
(Quoted in Hampton and Fayer, *Voices of Freedom*)

jacket) and guns than for its political programme.

In May 1967, BPP members carried their weapons into the California state parliament building to demonstrate against a proposed ban on the carrying of loaded weapons. This 'invasion' received widespread negative media coverage. The Panthers insisted that 'picking up the gun' was a political act designed to galvanize the black community, but the image of young black men openly carrying guns in the street antagonized the white establishment and placed the BPP on a collision course with the forces of law and order.

San Francisco, May 1967: a police lieutenant informs Black Panthers that they may keep their weapons, provided that they do not disturb the peace.

By late 1968, the BPP had chapters in 25 cities and was being described by the FBI as 'the greatest threat to the internal security of the country'. Blaming it for the violence following King's death, the police and the FBI set out to destroy the BPP. By 1970, with its leaders dead, jailed or exiled, the party had collapsed.

THE END OF THE CIVIL RIGHTS MOVEMENT 1966–68

The achievements of the civil rights movement – political and social equality for blacks – had galvanized the South, but they meant little to urban blacks in the North, who suffered from less obvious forms of racial discrimination. In the Northern cities blacks were crammed into segregated areas or ghettos, where they lived in run-down housing, went to run-down schools and worked in low-paid jobs. Unemployment (20-30 per cent), crime, drugs and gang warfare ravaged their communities, while insensitive policing fuelled their resentment and encouraged the growth of black militancy.

Five days after the Voting Rights Act was passed in August 1965, events in the Watts district of Los Angeles underlined the seriousness of racial inequality in American cities. A six-day riot left 34 people dead, 1,000 injured and over $40 million worth of damage. King publicly condemned the rioting, but he realized that the civil rights movement's next campaign should focus on the ghetto.

Riot damage, Los Angeles, 15 August 1965: the remains of a drive-in restaurant, seen through the broken window of another restaurant.

Chicago (1966)

In 1966, King and his followers went to Chicago to campaign against discrimination in employment and housing. They organized non-violent rallies, marches and demonstrations to force the city's powerful mayor 'Boss' Daley, to accept their demands. But the strategies that had worked so successfully in the South were inappropriate in Chicago, with its complex system of political patronage. There was an embarrassing lack of support for the marches, reflecting grassroots cynicism and the opposition of many of Chicago's black leaders.

The most effective tactic was to march through Chicago's white neighbourhoods, where the residents pelted the marchers with stones and bottles. This created a crisis when the deployment of Chicago's police to protect the marchers angered whites, who threatened to withdraw their vote. Daley called a summit and signed an agreement pledging to improve housing conditions. But too many powerful economic interests ensured that the promises were never kept.

Martin Luther King ducks as an object is thrown at the marchers in Chicago, 1966.

Boss Daley's plantation

Dorothy Tillman, an SCLC member who had worked on a voter registration project in the South before moving to Chicago, recalled the shock of confronting Daley's political machine and the black leaders who served it:

'Up here they lived on a plantation with Boss Daley as slave master. Their jobs, their clothes, their shelter, food, that all depended on Boss Daley. And everything was connected. Any little thing they did for you, you had to pay for it ... "Okay Mrs Jones ... now you go down here and vote for so and so". The six black aldermen [city councillors], they just nodded up and down and would deliver the black community.'
(Quoted in Hampton and Fayer, *Voices of Freedom*)

Failure in Chicago forced King to reassess his assumptions about American society. The howling white mobs revealed the roots of racism to be much deeper than he had thought. Their hatred was not the result of irrational prejudice, but fear of losing their economic advantage.

The Detroit riots (1967)

The Watts riots set a pattern. The explosive mixture of poor social and economic conditions, anger (at continual police harassment) and a small criminal element finally erupted into full-scale riots, which raged through dozens of American cities over three summers (1965-67).

Detroit, 1967: a policeman watches against sniper attack on firemen dealing with a blaze during the riots.

As the riots spread, the civil rights movement suffered. Images of black violence dominated the media, reinforcing a negative perception of black people out of control. In 1968, King

Like a carnival

Albert Wilson, who was 13 at the time, recalled his excitement during the riot and the permanent scars it left on him:

'I ... snuck out the back door ... It was kind of like a carnival ... because everyone there was laughing ... I had no sense of the danger ... we hear someone say, "The police are coming" ... so everyone finds a place to hide ... and I hear this police officer say, "... come out from back there". Well I immediately get up and head for the door ... when I hear a voice ... "Don't go out there. Come back." ... I went to turn to get back ... I just remember seeing a flash of light ... I woke up ... a couple of days later ... the bullet had injured my spine ... I was [permanently] paralysed."
(Quoted in Hampton and Fayer, *Voices of Freedom*)

They didn't know what to do

Roger Wilkins (nephew of the NAACP's director, Roy Wilkins) was director of the US Justice Department's Community Relations Service during the Detroit riots. He described the situation:

'We then met with Governor Romney, ... the head of the Michigan National Guard, and the police superintendent. They didn't know what to do ... When I made my rounds of the city at night, it was eerie. There was no traffic on the streets and the city was very dark ... There were armed checkpoints all over the city ... Occasionally there were gunshots, but invariably, when we checked them out, we found they came from some trigger-happy Guardsman ... danger in the streets ... came from the forces of law and order ... The Michigan Guard was made up of white country kids who didn't know the city and were scared of blacks ... and the Detroit Police had a long-standing reputation for brutality.'
(Quoted in Wilkins, *A Man's Life*)

warned the press that they were driving non-violent spokesmen like him to become more militant. 'If we don't say what you want, we don't get on the news. Who does? The militants ... you're making violence the way to publicize our cause.'

The worst riot occurred in Detroit, Michigan, in July 1967. It lasted a week, causing 43 deaths, 2,000 injured, 7,000 arrests and $45 million worth of damage. Paratroopers and tanks patrolled the streets and martial law was declared. Afterwards, President Johnson appointed a special commission to determine why the riots happened and how to prevent them happening again. Its report warned that the country was '... moving towards two societies, one black, one white – separate and unequal ... white society is deeply implicated in the ghetto. White institutions created it, white institutions maintain it and white society condones it.' Few of the recommendations were implemented and living conditions remained unchanged for most blacks.

The promised land

On 3 April 1968, King made his last great speech, reminding his supporters how far they had come:

'Well I don't know what will happen now. We've got some difficult days ahead. … I just want to do God's will. And he's allowed me to go up to the mountain. And I've looked over and I've seen the promised land. I may not get there with you. But I want you to know tonight, that we, as a people, will get to the promised land.'
(Quoted in Oates, *Let the Trumpet Sound*)

James Earl Ray (left), the convicted killer of Martin Luther King, is led from his prison block to give a television interview.

Martin Luther King's death (1968)

As a result of his experiences in Chicago and mounting criticism by Black Power supporters, King broadened the civil rights programme to address the causes of social and economic inequality. A committed pacifist, he started opposing the Vietnam War, especially for diverting essential funds from Johnson's social programme against poverty.

Hostile reactions to King's more radical outlook, from a coalition of Washington, white liberals, black conservatives and the press, led to a withdrawal of support. King appealed to the poor of all races to join a 'Poor People's Campaign' against poverty and unemployment, and unveiled plans for a mass tent-in in Washington to take place in May 1968.

But his plans were interrupted by a trip to Memphis, Tennessee, in spring 1968 to support a strike by black sanitation workers demanding equal pay. When the march deteriorated into fighting between young blacks and the police, King vowed to return and lead a second non-violent rally. However, on 4 April, he was killed by a sniper's bullet while standing on the balcony of his hotel. His assassin, James

People gather to watch a parade on Martin Luther King Day, in Miami, Florida.

Earl Ray, an escaped convict and Nazi, was later arrested and sentenced to 99 years in prison. As news of King's death spread, rioting exploded across the USA as angry mobs took to the streets in 110 cities.

Some 100,000 mourners attended King's funeral in Atlanta, where they sang the words of the old Negro spiritual: 'Free at last, free at last. Thank God Almighty, we are free at last!' King's contribution to American history was recognized twenty years later when he was given the unique honour of having his birthday commemorated as a public holiday.

A declaration of war

Stokely Carmichael echoed many people's views when he suggested that King's death would have violent repercussions. King was the only black leader that all factions within the black community would listen to:

'When America killed Dr King last night, she declared war on us. He was the one man in our race who was trying to teach our people to have love, compassion and mercy for white people.'
(Quoted in Hampton and Fayer, *Voices of Freedom*)

THE CIVIL RIGHTS LEGACY

After King's death, with no strong, central figure to hold the opposing forces together, the fragile coalition behind the civil rights movement unravelled. The Poor People's Campaign flopped through poor planning and a lack of media interest. Personality differences eventually split the squabbling SCLC and SNCC, leaving the NAACP as the country's largest and most influential civil rights group.

After 1968, the most visible sign of racial progress was the rise of black political power. By the 1990s, there were 40 black representatives in Congress and a black Supreme Court judge (Thurgood Marshall, architect of the NAACP's legal strategy against segregation). At state level, black mayors were elected in major cities throughout the USA, including Chicago (Harold Washington), Los Angeles (Thomas Bradley), New York (David Dinkins) and even Birmingham (Richard Arrington), site of one of the movement's greatest victories.

Female Democratic members of Congress pose on stage at the Democratic Convention, 2000.

Jesse Jackson (left), House Speaker Jim Wright and Rosa Parks sing 'We shall overcome' at a breakfast prayer meeting in 1988.

Blacks also formed powerful lobbying groups in Washington, preventing the achievements of the civil rights movement from being undermined by successive Republican administrations and campaigning for equal opportunities in employment and education.

Colin Powell, Secretary of State, 2001.

During the 1980s, the Reverend Jesse Jackson (a former SCLC organizer) showed how far civil rights had come when he became the first black person to challenge for the presidential candidacy. However, the first black person with a realistic chance of becoming president was General Colin Powell, a Gulf War hero. For personal reasons he declined to stand, but in 2001 he accepted a senior position in President George Bush's Republican administration.

Although greater educational and job opportunities have helped create a black middle class (comprising roughly half of the USA's 30 million blacks in 2000), two decades of civil rights progress cannot undo centuries of

No change in police attitudes

In 1994, Jean Carey Bond wrote to the *New York Times* about the kind of police behaviour that infuriated young black men:

'When my son … was a teenager, he was walking home after a school event when a police car screeched to a halt in front of him. Its doors flew open and four white cops jumped out, guns drawn. They threw him up against a wall, patted him down and grilled him, a gun at his head all the while. Fortunately for my son, a white classmate was passing and identified him to the cops. It seems a mugging had occurred in the area and my son fitted the description of the mugger – meaning my son was black.'
(*The New York Times*, November 1994)

oppression. An impoverished, neglected underclass inhabits the inner cities, where far more blacks than whites live below the poverty line.

Police brutality is also a major cause of racial discontent. In April 1992, riots in Los Angeles and other major cities started after four white policemen accused of savagely beating a black motorist, Rodney King, were acquitted of using 'excessive force' by an all-white jury, despite videotaped evidence. The riot lasted three days and was the worst civil disorder in American history – 51 people were killed, 2,000 injured and over $1 billion worth of property was damaged.

A burning home, during the 1992 riots in Los Angeles.

Affirmative action

After the Voting Rights Act (1965), the next stage in the battle for civil rights was the promotion of positive discrimination, or affirmative action (AA) – increasing employment and educational opportunities for blacks by reserving places (racial quotas) as compensation for past discrimination.

President Johnson rightly saw this as the next stage for achieving full civil rights, expressing his ideas to Washington's all-black Howard University in 1965: 'You do not take a person who for years has been hobbled by chains and liberate him, bring him up to the starting line of a race and then say, "You are free to compete with the others" ... We seek ... not just equality as a right ... but equality as a fact.'

In September that year, Johnson followed up words with actions when he issued Executive Order 11246 and set up the Office of Federal Contract Compliance (OFCC) to open up more skilled jobs to blacks and withhold federal money from any businesses that did not promote blacks within their organization. In 1971, the Supreme Court reinforced AA by approving the promotion of 'protected minorities' in Giggs v. Duke Power Co.

A problem of language

Mary Berry, who served in President Carter's administration as assistant secretary of education, explained the importance of affirmative action for black progress:

'... when you start talking about affirmative action as being "preferential treatment", you have already set up a situation where anybody who is the beneficiary of preferential treatment will lose. If you say "reverse discrimination" against somebody, it already sounds like a bad thing is happening and you don't focus on what injustice was. So affirmative action was not preferential treatment for blacks. What it was, was trying to do something about remedying preferential treatment for whites, the injustice that had occurred in the past.' (Quoted in Hampton and Fayer, *Voices of Freedom*)

Newly elected mayor of Atlanta, Maynard Jackson, and his wife, Bunie.

In 1973, Atlanta, Georgia, elected the first Southern black mayor, Maynard Jackson, who promoted an aggressive AA programme. He increased the number of black employees at all levels of local government, including the police force, and ensured that around one-third of the city's business contracts, including the redevelopment of the airport, went to black-run companies.

Black leaders realized that AA programmes would not be effective if blacks lacked the necessary qualifications to apply for university places or skilled jobs. In 1969 the Supreme Court ordered the immediate desegregation of all public schools (many states had delayed integration before then). Within five years, the proportion of black children in segregated schools had dropped from 68 per cent to 8 per cent, and Southern schools soon became the most integrated in the USA.

Making history

Phyllis Ellison was a black student bused to a previously all-white school. She recalled the sacrifices involved in making a stand for equal education:

'I remember my first day going on the bus to South Boston High School ... We had police escorts ... you could hear people saying, "Niggers go home." ... there were people on the corners holding bananas like we were apes, monkeys ... On a normal day there would be anywhere between 10 and 15 fights ... at that time there was so much tension in the school that one fight would have the school dismissed for the entire day ... inside the classroom ... the black students sat on one side ... the white students sat on the other side ... we attended the same school, but we never really did anything together.'
(Quoted in Hampton and Fayer, *Voices of Freedom*)

Many Northern schools remained segregated by geography (separate racial neighbourhoods) rather than law. In 1971 the Supreme Court resolved this problem by authorising a busing policy to take white children to inner-city black schools and vice versa. Many whites protested, some even setting the school buses on fire. The loudest and longest resistance came from Boston, where white protestors formed ROAR (Restore Our Alienated Rights) in 1974 to 'protect their community', using boycotts, demonstrations and intimidation. Despite a lack of political support for busing, ROAR eventually faded away.

Black students are bused home from school in South Boston, under heavy police guard, September 1974.

120 people in one room!

In an account of his experiences teaching in a black neighbourhood school in Boston during the 1960s, Jonathan Kozol describes typical working conditions:

'The room in which I taught my Fourth Grade was not a room at all, but the corner of an auditorium … Over at the other end of the auditorium was another fourth Grade class … It became a real nightmare of conflicting noises … by ten thirty it would have attained such a crescendo that the children in the back rows … often could not hear my questions and I could not hear their answers … Soon after I discovered that … we were to share the space … with play rehearsals, special reading, special arithmetic … Once I counted 120 people in the one room.'
(Quoted in Kozol, *Death at an Early Age*)

By the late 1970s, AA was also being attacked, with whites complaining that quotas were a form of 'reverse discrimination'. The most important challenge came with the case of the Regents of the University of California v. Bakke (1978). Bakke, a white engineer, claimed he had been unfairly denied admission (twice) to the university's medical school, because of its AA programme. A divided Supreme Court agreed, ruling that minority quotas were unconstitutional where they denied 'equal rights for all'.

During the 1980s, President Ronald Reagan withdrew federal support from thousands of AA and welfare programmes. This coincided with a downturn in economic prosperity, when improving opportunities for blacks were seen to threaten white job security and living standards. During the 1990s, the Supreme Court restricted AA programmes to cases where prior racial discrimination could be proved. In 1996, California became the first state to ban AA programmes.

People outside the court house in Los Angeles react to the 'not guilty' verdict in the O. J. Simpson murder case, October 1995.

Ironically, considering its troubled history of segregation, the USA's greatest equal opportunity employer today is the armed services, with a larger proportion of blacks in positions of authority than any other public organization.

A ceaseless struggle

The USA's continuing racial polarization was illustrated by the O. J. Simpson murder trial in 1995. Simpson, a famous black American football star and actor, was accused of murdering his white wife and her friend. After an eight-month televised trial, a mainly black jury acquitted him. However, opinions on Simpson's guilt were divided along racial lines: most whites found him guilty, most blacks found him innocent. When Simpson was found guilty at a later civil trial, it seemed that the country had managed the impossible: a verdict to satisfy each race.

During Black History Month, February 2001, President George Bush Jr, reads from a book about Booker T. Washington to a school class in Washington DC. Unlike the previous president, Bill Clinton, the Republican George Bush (elected in 2000) was not popular with black voters.

However, this should not overshadow the extraordinary achievements of the men and women who made the civil rights movement a true mass movement, representing not just the hopes and dreams of a race, but the principles of equality on which American democracy had been built. Together, black and white, young and old, lawyer and labourer, they struggled for freedom's cause. Together they wrote a new chapter of American history, changing American society forever.

A ceaseless struggle

Howard Zinn, a professor of political science at Boston University and former SNCC activist, evaluated the legacy of the civil rights movement:

'I believe the most important thing that Americans can learn from the civil rights movement is that ... democracy is not fulfilled by going through the "proper channels" of representative government, and that democracy only becomes alive when citizens unite to ... create a movement which arouses the conscience of society. Democracy ... requires a ceaseless struggle, involving sacrifice and risk.'
(Quoted in Wexler, *The Civil Rights Movement: An Eyewitness History*)

DATE LIST

1619	Black slaves first arrive in America, at Jamestown, Virginia.
1776-83	American War of Independence.
1845	Frederick Douglass publishes his influential *Narrative and Life of an American Slave*.
1861-65	American Civil War.
1863	Emancipation Proclamation frees all slaves in rebel states.
1866, 1869, 1870	Civil Rights Act; 14th and 15th amendments to the Constitution.
1890s	Establishment of 'Jim Crow' laws across Southern states.
1896	Plessy v. Ferguson gives constitutional backing for segregation.
1909	Formation of the National Association for the Advancement of Coloured People (NAACP).
1915-25	'Great Migration' leads to influx of blacks into Northern cities.
1916	Formation of Universal Negro Improvement Association (UNIA) by Marcus Garvey.
1919	'Red Summer' of rioting across 25 cities, including Chicago.
1930	Formation of Nation of Islam (NOI) in Detroit.
1941	President Roosevelt bans racial discrimination in the defence industries after pressure from labour leader A. Philip Randolph.
1942	Formation of Congress of Racial Equality (CORE) in Chicago.
1948	President Truman abolishes segregation in the armed forces.

1954	Brown v. Topeka Board of Education outlaws segregation in schools.
1955	Lynching of Emmet Louis Till in Money, Mississippi. Rosa Parks arrested for refusing to give up her bus seat to a white man, Montgomery, Alabama.
1956	Montgomery Bus Boycott results in ban on segregated seating. Formation of Southern Christian Leadership Conference (SCLC).
1957	President Eisenhower orders federal troops to enforce school desegregation at Little Rock, Arkansas.
1960	Four black students stage first sit-in, Greensboro, North Carolina. Formation of Student Non-violent Coordinating Committee (SNCC). Supreme Court outlaws segregation in interstate bus terminals.
1961	CORE-sponsored 'freedom rides' test interstate desegregation across South; ICC enforces desegregation.
1961-62	First civil rights setback in Albany, Georgia, during campaign for desegregation of town's facilities.
1962	Formation of Council of Federated Organizations (COFO); launch of voter registration drive in South.
1963	Civil rights victory in Birmingham, Alabama, after police attack marching children with dogs and fire hoses. Huge civil rights demonstration in Washington DC. President Kennedy assassinated.

1964	'Freedom Summer' voter registration programme and formation of Mississippi Freedom Democratic Party (MFDP). Civil Rights Act passed (July). Martin Luther King awarded Nobel Peace Prize.		**1966 cont.**	SCLC campaign in Chicago. Black Power slogan first used during 'March against Fear'.
1964-68	Racial violence in over 200 cities during five long, 'hot' summers.		**1967**	Thurgood Marshall becomes first black Supreme Court Justice; and Carl Stokes first black mayor of major US city – Cleveland, Ohio. Rioting in Detroit.
1965	Demonstrations for voter rights in Selma, Alabama, attract public support of President Johnson. Assassination of Malcolm X. Voting Rights Act passed (July). Formation of first black political party: Lowndes County Freedom Organization (LCFO). Rioting in Watts district, LA.		**1968**	King's assassination leads to mass rioting in over 100 cities.
			1973-80	Maynard Jackson elected mayor of Atlanta, Georgia; implements Affirmative Action programme.
			1992	Rioting in LA after white police found not guilty of using excessive force against a black motorist.
1966	Formation of Black Panther Party (BPP) in Oakland, California.		**2001**	General Colin Powell appointed Secretary of State, becoming most senior black figure in US history.

RESOURCES

H. Brogan, *The Penguin History of the USA* (Penguin, 1985) includes good background to race relations.

F. Douglass, *Narrative of the Life of Frederick Douglass, an American Slave* (HUP 1854/1967) is a powerful autobiography of America's first black leader.

A. Haley, *Autobiography of Malcolm X* (Grove Press, 1965); publication of this detailed account helped to turn him into an icon of black radicalism.

H. Hampton and S. Fayer, *Voices of Freedom* (Vintage, 1990), transcribed from a TV series, *Eyes on the Prize*, is a wide-ranging oral history of the civil rights struggle.

A. Moody, *Coming of Age in Mississippi* (Dial Press, 1968) is the moving autobiography of a black woman who worked with CORE and the NAACP.

S. Oates, *Let the Trumpet Sound* (Harper & Row, 1982) is a highly readable biography of Martin Luther King.

S. Wexler, *The Civil Rights Movement: An Eyewitness History* (Facts on File, 1993) covers each of the main events between 1865 and 1965 with potted histories, chronologies and eyewitness testimony.

Fiction and films

Uncle Tom's Cabin (1852) by Harriet Beecher Stowe was written in reaction to the punitive 1850 Fugitive Slave Act (which assumed all blacks accused of being runaway slaves to be guilty). The novel was a sensational success and helped to stir up public feeling.

To Kill a Mockingbird (1960) by Harper Lee is a classic tale of racial prejudice, about a white lawyer defending a black man falsely accused of raping a white girl.

Norman Jewison's film *In the Heat of the Night* (1967) is a thriller which explores racism through the clashing personalities of a black New York detective and a white sheriff jointly investigating a murder in the South.

Malcolm X (1992) by Spike Lee is a lengthy, absorbing biopic by a radical black director; it tries hard not to offend, and mainly ignores Malcolm's ambiguous relationship with the civil rights movement.

Visit www.learn.co.uk for more resources

GLOSSARY

Attorney General   the US president's chief legal adviser.

Black Power   the slogan behind black consciousness, designed to promote social equality and racial pride.

boycott   to refuse to deal with an organization or a process, in order to force a change of policy.

civil rights   political and human rights protected by the constitution, that all citizens are supposed to have – e.g. the rights to vote, to equal use of public facilities, to equal treatment before the law, and to freedom of speech.

Congress   the national law-making body of the USA, consisting of the House of Representatives (435 members) and the Senate (100 members).

constitution   a statement of the basic laws and principles by which a country or organization is governed. The US constitution (created in 1789) has seven articles and 26 amendments. Judicial decisions often guide its interpretation.

direct action   a political or industrial action, such as a strike, boycott or civil disobedience, designed to have an immediate effect on influencing a government or employer.

discrimination   singling out minority or other groups for unfavourable treatment.

FBI (Federal Bureau of Investigation)   a bureau of the US Department of Justice that deals with matters of national security and interstate crime.

federal government   in the USA, the central government, which is responsible for national foreign policy, military policy, taxation and welfare. State governments (there are 50) retain limited self-government and can raise local taxes and draft their own laws. In case of dispute, the judiciary decides between the two authorities.

Gandhi   Mohandas Gandhi (1869-1948) was the leader of the Indian independence movement against British colonial rule. He promoted non-violent direct action to achieve his goals.

ghetto   an area of a city lived in by a minority group, often run-down and densely populated.

grassroots   formed by and involving ordinary people from a community or an organization.

integration   mixing blacks and whites where they were previously segregated.

lynch mob   group of people who seize and kill someone (usually by hanging) without legal arrest and trial, because they think the person has committed a crime.

Marxism   a political ideology based on the theories of Karl Marx and Friedrich Engels; it identifies class struggle as a necessary part of social change.

National Guard   military reserve units equipped by the federal government, but under state control; can be called into service by either federal or state governments.

Negro   term commonly used by both blacks and whites before the 1970s to describe African Americans. It is now considered offensive.

plantation   large estate where crops such as cotton or tobacco are grown; labourers usually live on the estate.

segregation   enforced separation of racial groups, especially through the use of separate schools, housing, transport and other facilities

Supreme Court   the highest federal court in the USA, consisting of nine justices (judges) appointed by the president; the court rules on constitutional matters.

INDEX

SOURCES

Sources for this book were:

Carson, Claybourne et al (ed.), *The Eyes on the Prize: A Civil Rights Reader*, Viking Penguin, 1991

Cook, Robert, *Sweet Land of Liberty*, Addison Wesley Longman, 1998

Hampton, Henry & Fayer, Steve, *Voices of Freedom: An Oral History of the Civil Rights Movement from the 1950s through the 1980s*, Vintage, 1995

Johnson, Jacqueline, *Stokely Carmichael: The Story of Black Power*, Silver Burdett Press, 1990

Kelly, Nigel (ed.), *Black Peoples of the Americas*, Heinemann, 1998

Kozol, Jonathan, *Death at an Early Age*, Houghton Mifflin, 1967

Moody, Anne, *Coming of Age in Mississippi*, Doubleday & Co, 1968

Oates, Stephen, *Let the Trumpet Sound: The Life of Martin Luther King, Jr*, Search Press, 1982

Wexler, Sanford, *The Civil Rights Movement: An Eyewitness History*, Facts on File, Inc., 1993

Wilkins, Roger, *A Man's Life: An Autobiography*, Simon and Schuster, 1982